Anybody Can Sell

Practical Tips to Master the Art of Selling

Subramanian Chandramouli

INDIA • SINGAPORE • MALAYSIA

Notion Press

Old No. 38, New No. 6
McNichols Road, Chetpet
Chennai - 600 031

First Published by Notion Press 2018
Copyright © Subramanian Chandramouli 2018
All Rights Reserved.

ISBN 978-1-64249-865-3

This book has been published with all reasonable efforts taken to make the material error-free after the consent of the author. No part of this book shall be used, reproduced in any manner whatsoever without written permission from the author, except in the case of brief quotations embodied in critical articles and reviews.

The Author of this book is solely responsible and liable for its content including but not limited to the views, representations, descriptions, statements, information, opinions and references ["Content"]. The Content of this book shall not constitute or be construed or deemed to reflect the opinion or expression of the Publisher or Editor. Neither the Publisher nor Editor endorse or approve the Content of this book or guarantee the reliability, accuracy or completeness of the Content published herein and do not make any representations or warranties of any kind, express or implied, including but not limited to the implied warranties of merchantability, fitness for a particular purpose. The Publisher and Editor shall not be liable whatsoever for any errors, omissions, whether such errors or omissions result from negligence, accident, or any other cause or claims for loss or damages of any kind, including without limitation, indirect or consequential loss or damage arising out of use, inability to use, or about the reliability, accuracy or sufficiency of the information contained in this book.

Contents

Acknowledgments   *v*

Why this book?   *vii*

Preparing for a meeting   1

Cold call   5

Lead generation   13

How to find the right prospect   25

Questioning   35

Proposal writing   43

Pricing for profit   51

Response time as competitive strategy   61

Cross selling and up selling   69

Negotiation   75

Objection handling   81

CONTENTS

Closing the sale	89
Effective networking	95
Handling internal teams	103
Follow up	109
Power of asking	115
Referrals and feedback	123
Gratitude	127
Reference books	*131*

ACKNOWLEDGMENTS

I would like to thank my wife Vidya who has patiently supported me all throughout my entrepreneurial journey. My mother Vijaya who always prays for my well-being. Gomathi and Ramesh who stood by me during the tough days of my life. Sundar, Ilangkumaran, Sindhu and Jaya who gave their unconditional support without any expectations.

Paritosh and AK Kannan from whom I learnt sales during the initial part of my career. My good friends Ramesh Sigamani, Rajanikanth, Sapna and Jinoo who constantly convinced me to choose a career in sales training. My friend Smitha who helped me with proof reading and editing.

Special thanks to my mentor Srinivasan Ranganathan Co-Founder, Inside-Out Foundation, who guided me onto the right path.

WHY THIS BOOK?

I conduct sales training across India and Middle East. I have come across many entrepreneurs who are very strong in their domain and functional areas but lack sales skills. They have a strong fear of sales. The objective of this book is to erase the fear of sales from their minds and help them to use simple tools and concepts which will make sales easy for them.

Also young people who start their career in sales need to know the fundamentals of sales. This book will be a guide to them. All the topics discussed here will help them understand the topic easily, and the practical examples given in each chapter will enable them to connect with the situations they face in their lives.

PREPARING FOR A MEETING

Ramesh Sigamani is a wealth advisor who runs a company called Bravisa Temple Tree. He handles the wealth of ultra-high networth individuals. After 6 months of follow-up, he got the opportunity to meet a highly reputed businessman. If Ramesh convinces the businessman to invest with him, he will get a portfolio worth tens of crores. Ramesh wants to prepare for this meeting in the best possible way.

Now, let's put a structure to prepare for such meetings. Before every customer meeting, you should have 3 objectives in your mind. This is irrespective of whether you are meeting the customer for the first time or after submitting a proposal or any other similar situation. The 3 objectives are:

1. Primary Objective (PO)
2. Secondary Objective 1 (SO 1)
3. Secondary Objective 2 (SO 2)

So now, the question in your mind is, what should your primary objective be? How should you define your primary objective?

Many sales people follow the SMART way of setting goals. SMART stands for

S – Specific

M – Measurable

A – Action Oriented

R – Realistic

T – Time Bound

In general, your primary objective (PO) should be to close the deal. In sales terminology, it is called Always Be Closing or ABC. But in reality, closure is not always possible on the first meeting.

The below table will help you to prepare primary and secondary objectives.

S.No	Example	Primary Objective	Secondary Objective 1	Secondary Objective 2
1	You are selling computer servers to corporates, and you are meeting the client for the	Get the client's approval to send a proposal to him within next 2 days for selling 15	Get an appointment for next Monday for giving a demonstration to the technical	Get connected with the divisional head who will be the user/ stakeholder

	first time.	servers.	team on the various products that can be provided.	for your product/ service.
2	You are an architect and are meeting a commercial land owner for the first time. He wants to build a commercial complex.	Get the client's approval to send a proposal within a week for building a commercial complex, along with costing and approximate time of completion.	Get an appointment for next Friday to take the client for a tour on his/her earlier projects where the customer can see his/her work in person.	Get an appointment for the next meeting which should happen within next one week.

If you are able to achieve the Primary Objective, it means the following:

- The customer is interested in working with you
- He/she believes that you have the ability to do the work
- Customer has not taken a decision yet about whether to award the project to you or not, but is interested in exploring options

If you are not able to achieve the Primary Objective, you should try to achieve SO 1, and if you still can't achieve it, you should focus on achieving SO 2. Without achieving it, you should not leave the meeting room.

How will this plan help you? This plan, when written in paper, gives you a clear idea of what you want to achieve from this meeting. Your entire discussion will be based on this. Without this written plan, you will be just answering the questions your customer is asking.

This plan has helped me immensely in meetings.

Key Takeaways:

- Before every meeting or a customer call, have a clear plan
- The plan should have Primary Objective, Secondary Objective 1 and Secondary Objective 2
- Objective should be written using SMART framework
- Without achieving Primary or Secondary Objectives, you should not leave the meeting room

COLD CALL

Sapna is a commercial photographer and one of her specializations is food photography. She wants to expand her business. Recently she attended an exhibition and bought a book with the contact details of all the major restaurants in the city. She thought she should do a cold call to all the restaurants and ask them whether they have displayed good photos in their website or in the food review websites. But she is worried whether cold calls will work in this mobile app era.

Many participants in my workshop have asked me whether cold calls would work in today's world. My perception is cold calling still works. But the difference is, we are no longer contacting a person with absolutely no idea. Everybody is in the social media space. So the moment we get a contact, we do some research on the internet and understand what kind of a person he or she is and then make an informed cold call. In my understanding, uninformed cold calls have changed to informed cold calls.

If you want to make a cold call, the below mentioned pointers will help you.

- In a cold call, your first 12–15 words are very important. Don't waste that in telling about who you are, where you are from and how good your product is etc. Nobody is interested in listening to that. The other party is only interested in what **benefit** he/she will get from you or your product or service.

- When you are making that cold call, do you think the other party is waiting near the phone to eagerly receive the call? Absolutely not! The human brain processes more than 60,000 ideas in a day. When somebody answers your call, his/her mind is already thinking of 100 different things. So, your first goal is to bring his/her focus toward you. Hence, your first 12–15 words are very important.

So, what are those first 12–15 words? Before going there, let's understand why people buy. If you are in a Business to Business (B2B) business, customers will buy only if the following objectives are met:

- Is your product or service helping them to increase their revenue?
- Is your product or service helping them to decrease their cost?

So, if you are making a cold call and you are in a B2B business, you should address any of the above 2 questions in your first 12–15 words. For example:

Good Morning, Sir. I am Aniruddh from XYZ Enterprise. We help our clients increase their revenue by 20% every quarter.

Then your prospective customer will be interested to know how you do that. Then you start talking about the benefits of your product or service and request an appointment for a face-to-face meeting to discuss in detail.

Remember, the moment the client is asking you how, he/she is ready to listen to you. You have earned the right for next 60 seconds of his/her time.

Some more examples:

Good Morning, Sir. I am Aniruddh from XYZ Enterprise. We help our clients reduce their IT cost by 15% every quarter.

Good Morning, Sir. I am Krishna from ABC Solutions. We help our clients reduce their manpower cost by 15% every quarter.

Good Morning, Sir. I am Krishna from ABC Solutions. We help our clients increase their employee productivity by 25% over 6 months.

And be prepared to tell the logic of how you will increase employee productivity by 25% over 6 months. You should be well-prepared and should be honest with it.

Now if you are in a Business to Consumer (B2C) business, then what should be your first 12-15 words over the call?

B2C customers buy things only for 2 reasons.

1. How will your product or service help them achieve their goal?
2. How will your product or service help them solve their challenges?

Say for example, if you are running a beauty parlor, you are in the business of helping them achieve their goal of looking good. Your first 12-15 words in the call should be:

Good Morning, Madam. I am Sindhu from ABC Wellness Solutions. We help our clients gain self-confidence and help them achieve their goal within 3 months.

When the prospective customer asks you how you are doing it, then you answer that you have a 3 month grooming program, where you improve their image with various beauty tips and make them feel confident and happy about themselves.

Some more examples:

If you are running a restaurant, then you are in the business of helping them solve the problem of cooking their food. Address this in your first 12–15 words of your call.

Good Morning, Sir. I am Sindhu from Krishna Restaurant. We help our clients live a healthy and happy life by saving their time by 20% every month.

Now, some of you may have a question, "If we are calling through the board, how do we get connected to the right person?" I will give you an example.

> Rajeev Kumar is a Sales Manager working in a reputed e-learning company.
>
> One fine day, when he was free, he searched Google for top 10 e-learning companies of India.

> He wanted to partner with them and get some projects to outsource. He got a list of 10 companies and started calling each one of them through the board. His pitch was simple and powerful.
>
> *I am Rajeev, Director of XYZ E-learning Solutions. We have a business proposition for your company. Can you please connect me to your Content Head?*
>
> The receptionist responded by saying they don't encourage calls from unknown people.
>
> Rajeev replied, "*We have a business proposition and if your company is not interested, I don't mind. We will give this to other e-learning companies.*
>
> *Thanks.*"
>
> Immediately, receptionist connected him to the content head.

If you start requesting the receptionist to connect you to the content head, you will never get connected. The confidence and the tone of your voice determines whether you get connected to the right person or not. It's not about what you say, it's all about how you say.

Key Takeaways:

- In this digital era, cold calls have become informed cold calls. Still it's worth giving a shot.

- In any cold call, your opening statement is most important.

- In your opening statement, your first 12-15 words earn you the right for next 60 seconds.

- In B2B business, always talk about increasing the revenue or decreasing the cost in your first 12-15 words.

- In B2C business, always talk about how you can help them in achieving their goal or solving their problems.

- When you are doing a cold call through board line, the way you put your message to the receptionist will decide whether you get connected to the right person or not.

LEAD GENERATION

Jinoo is a real estate consultant. She connects the buyers and sellers to buy or sell land parcels, flats and independent houses. Currently, she generates leads through online portals which are focused on real estate transactions. But those leads are also passed to many other consultants like her. Her own contacts are very limited. She wants to think of other ways for generating leads.

One of the important problems every business faces is generating leads. How do you generate quality leads that will lead to business? There are multiple ways to generate leads.

Cold Call

As we discussed in the previous chapter, cold calling is one of the ways to generate leads. The only difference between a traditional cold call and today's cold call is, you can get the basic information of the person you are calling by doing just a Google search and read about them on Facebook or LinkedIn. There is no denying that with cold call also you can generate leads.

Social Media

In this digital era, you can definitely generate leads using social media. I know many small businesses which use Facebook as their only strategy to generate leads. If you are in B2C segment, Facebook is a good option as you can target your specific customers in a particular city, particular area, and for a particular time period. LinkedIn is another good option for other set of business customers. Based on your budget, you can create ads for your product or service. Even without making any investments, if you effectively use Facebook and LinkedIn, you can reach out to many potential customers. I recommend you attend Good Social Media Marketing Seminar and learn the tips and best practices to generate leads.

Networking Forums

Every entrepreneur or sales executive should be part of at least 3 forums which can generate continuous leads for them. BNI, Rotary, CII etc, are such good forums. If you attend these networking forums week on week, or biweekly or monthly as per their schedule, you will come across people who attend regularly.

After a few meetings, you will build a relationship which will help you in getting leads. The most important aspect in going to a networking forum is you have to be visible there. Just going to the forum will not help. You have to take volunteer positions and be visible to each and every member. Take part in a lot of activities so that everybody knows you. Genuinely be a go-to person for everybody there. We will discuss more on how to do networking in the chapters to follow.

Referrals from Existing Customers

Another best way to generate leads is to ask your existing customers for references. Once you provide quality service to an existing customer, you can ask him whether he can connect you to two people who may need your product or service. Definitely, they will be happy to connect them with you. You can ask this only after giving them a great service. You have to earn that right. Imagine you have 50 customers; just by doing this exercise, you would have created 100 prospective leads referred by a genuine business person. Keep this as a quarterly activity and once in 3 months, you can ask your existing customers for more references. There is nothing wrong in asking.

Print and Other Media

If you have the budget, you can think about advertising in print and other media like TV and radio. But you have to be very clear about the return on investment. It is better to do it through a reputed advertising agency that is familiar with the industry. I know a few companies who use the leading daily newspaper as their main referral generating engine to run their business. Nothing is right or wrong. You have to try what is working for you and stick to it. But you have to be very careful on the return on investment.

FRIENDS

I hope many of you know this FRIENDS acronym of lead generation. FRIENDS stands for:

F – Friends

R – Relatives

I – Institutions you studied

E – Employers (Current and ex employers)

N – Neighbors

D – Doctors (Meaning Professionals like Doctors, Lawyers, Auditors etc)

S – Strangers

Friends

We always spend time with our friends and never talk about business. Now we have WhatsApp groups for different kinds of friends we have, like cricket friends, school friends, college friends etc. Are we asking any specific referrals from them? You don't know what kind of connections they have. If you ask them to connect you to *anybody* who needs business, you are not going to get anything. You have to be very specific.

Specific is terrific. First, identify whom do you want to get connected to. Find the company name and if possible the exact person in that company. Say for example, you want to get connected to the procurement head of Google, then ask your friends through WhatsApp whether anybody can connect you to MR. ABC, the procurement head of Google. Who knows! One of your friends will be playing badminton every week with the procurement head of Google. Just keep asking your friends' network.

Relatives

We attend many family functions. Each one of us has a lot of relatives. But we hesitate to ask our relatives anything with respect to our business or profession. If you are a sales executive or an entrepreneur, you should come out of this mindset. After a general discussion with your relative during a family gathering, there is nothing wrong in asking for a specific connection or similar connections he/she would have. You may not get it immediately, but with the right and regular follow up, you have a chance of getting it. We have so many relatives. If you are able to tap into that network using your WhatsApp or any other social media, you have created another new set of referral generating engines for you and your company.

Institutions

All of us studied in a school or a college. Some of us would have studied UG and PG courses in different colleges. Some of us would have studied a foreign language course, or learnt any other extracurricular skill. And everywhere we have friends. Are we leveraging this network? Are you asking for specific referrals when you meet these friends? Are you using WhatsApp groups to ask your specific ask with these networks? Think about it. Alumni functions are a great way to bond and indirectly the best way to generate leads.

Employer

In our lifetime, we work with 5 to 6 companies or even more. We have different Facebook, LinkedIn and WhatsApp groups with our ex colleagues. Those colleagues would have also joined different companies by this time. They would have developed a new set of contacts. Are you leveraging them to get leads for you? Meet them once in a while. Be active in the groups. They can give you a lot of referrals if you have a specific ask.

Neighbors

Today, most of us live in an apartment or we have friends who live in an apartment. Each apartment has anywhere between 100 to 500 houses. We have to build a relationship with our neighboring community and you can ask them for referrals. It will be a great source of lead generation. I have seen many entrepreneurs getting excellent leads from their apartment community. You can also leverage the apartment community of your close friends. Everybody in that community works for a company. If you have 100 units in your apartment, you have 100 potential companies to target. All you have to do is some research and find out which company will be a potential customer for you.

Doctors

I use the word Doctors to fill the Acronym. By Doctors, I mean professionals. We deal with many self-employed professionals like Doctors, Lawyers, Auditors, and Dentists etc. They will have more contacts. Are we leveraging their network? Next time when you pay the doctor, ask for a referral, close the business and make money out of it. Going to a clinic may generate a lead for you. It's all about how we are asking. We will discuss about the power of asking in the upcoming chapter.

Strangers

Today, we all travel by flight, train and bus. We come across so many people. We are hesitant to have a conversation with them. Smart sales people are good in initiating a conversation. Once you are familiar with the stranger, you can ask for their business card or contact details and for specific referrals. You can also offer to help them in any way possible from your contacts. If you are genuinely willing to help people, definitely you are going to get the help back. What goes around, comes around. Many of my sales friends have got business from the strangers they have met in flights and trains. Never miss an opportunity.

Leads from News

Many sales executives ignore reading newspapers and magazines. Smart sales people know how to get business from a news item.

One of my friends, who is a very good Sales Manager, works for a renowned IT Services company. One day, he read an interview in a business newspaper. It featured an interview with India location head of a very prominent Fortune 100 global company. He talked about growth within the next 3 years and about the key important leaders who worked in the center.

My friend, being smart, noted all the details. His company, being the IT Services partner, had access to the organizational structure of the client. He went through all the names given in the interview and drilled down to their reporting executives and their teams and got all the contact details and their areas of interest. With this list, he sat down with his business unit head and created a sales strategy on where and how he can position his company for IT services.

Then he called all his potential customers and set up a meeting. Within 6 months of effort, he closed business worth INR 2 crores with them. Just by reading a news article, 2 crores worth of business was done!

I recommend you to read the business newspaper daily. If you are into recruitment, you should look for companies opening new development centers or getting VC funding. Then use your contacts or social media to reach the right person. When I was running my recruitment company, I used to read many newspapers and get business out of it.

For any business, there are a good number of leads waiting, provided you read news articles every single day and make efforts to reach out to the right person and close the deal diligently.

Another important point is that lead generation should be a continuous process. Whether you already have more business or not, you should never stop working to get more leads. You never know when leads will dry up. The market thumb rule is you will close only 20% of your leads. Say for example, if you have 20 leads currently, then most probably you will get only 4 closed deals out of it. So, the golden rule is: ***Always keep your funnel full***. Funnel should be full with your leads.

Key Takeaways:

- We can generate leads through multiple channels

- Cold call, social media, print, TV, radio are some of the channels

- BNI, CII and other networking forums are also good for lead generation

- You should always have a lead generation strategy in place

- FRIENDS framework will help you to generate more leads

- Newspapers, magazines and news articles are a great source of lead generation

- Lead generation should be a continuous process irrespective of whether you are doing good in your business or not

- The golden rule is "Always have more leads"

HOW TO FIND THE RIGHT PROSPECT

In one insurance company, there was this one sales guy called Aniruddh who won the Best Sales Person of the Year award continuously for 5 years. Everybody wanted to know how he was able to do it year on year. Even the chairman of the company wanted to know the secret. So, the chairman requested Aniruddh to share the secret with his colleagues.

Some people thought Aniruddh was very intelligent, some people thought Aniruddh was not ethical, others thought he was naturally gifted. But the truth was different. Everyone was waiting for Aniruddh's speech.

In his speech, Aniruddh told that his only secret is he spent most of his time with right prospects, whereas many of his colleagues spent time with all prospects. Now let's decode in detail the wisdom Aniruddh shared with us.

Selling in general has three major stages.

1. Prospect
2. Presentation
3. Follow up

Whenever your sales is down, if you concentrate only on these 3 things, then you can improve your sales quickly. You have to analyze which out of these 3 is weak for you at a particular time. The first part is the prospect. Once you generate many leads, you should filter your right prospect.

Imagine this basic model as a funnel; on top of the funnel, you put all your prospects. Then you filter prospects according to certain parameters. You have to call, mail, or WhatsApp certain number of people, who will agree to meet you in person or to whom you can present your products or service. Let's assume this ratio as 1:5. You call 25 people and 5 people agree to meet you. So you are meeting 5 people and giving presentation and 2 are interested in your service or product. As a next step, you follow up with these 2 people and one is buying from you. So, to make one sale, you have to call or get connected with 25 people. So, the golden rule is **keep your funnel full.**

80% of your time should be spent in prospecting and presenting and 20% of your time should be spent in follow up. So, another golden rule is **spend more time with better prospects**.

The definition of good prospect is *someone who will buy and pay within a reasonable period of time.*

In a larger context, you have to analyze only 2 important things.

1. Whether your prospect has MONEY
2. Whether he/she has the AUTHORITY to buy

Don't waste time with nice people who don't have the above 2 things. Most sales people waste their time by spending time with people who don't have the authority or money to buy.

I heard about one person who started enquiring about interior design for his house. One of my friends, an interior designer, met him at his office and explained about various designs and the approximate cost. During the next meeting, he showed him more designs and finally when my friend asked him to take him to his house, the prospect said that he was yet to buy a house and was looking out for various options.

Here, in this example my friend wasted his time and energy on a wrong prospect. He didn't apply the golden rule on **whether the prospect is willing to buy within a reasonable time frame**. Now you can question me how to find that. In the following sections of this book, you will find a chapter on questioning skills. By asking the right questions in the early stages of sales cycle, you can find the answer for it.

To quote another example, one of friends was selling an apartment. This prospect came along with his wife and inspected the flat. He was happy with it and asked for certain modifications which my friend agreed. During the next meeting, he also started negotiating on the price. When that was done, then finally he said, his father in law would come and decide whether to buy this flat or not. My friend had already spent 3 weeks with him and blocked this apartment for this particular prospect. Precious 3 weeks of selling time got lost. As an intelligent sales person, we should identify who the decision making authority on this transaction is. We can also find that by asking the right questions to the prospective buyer.

Qualities of a Good Prospect

1. Prospect has a genuine need that your product or service can fulfill

2. Prospect is friendly toward you and has a favorable impression of your company
3. Prospect values the results/benefits of what you sell more than the amount you charge
4. Prospect is willing and will be able to make a buying decision in the near future
5. Prospect is a good source of future sales and referrals

Let's discuss each one of them:

Genuine Need

The first thing we have to identify is whether the prospect has genuine need or not and whether our product or service will fulfill that need or not. Some prospects will be window shopping. If you go to any small textile shop, the shop keeper there will identify whether you are a window shopper or you have a genuine need within minutes. Just by asking you 2-3 questions and observing your body language, he/she will find that out. Then the shop keeper will not spend much time with you because he/she knows that the customer is not going to make a sale with you. Whatever business you are into, you have to improve this skill. Otherwise you will be wasting your precious time.

Friendly Favorable Impression

The next parameter to consider is how the prospect behaves with you. I am not saying that if the prospect doesn't display a positive behavior drop him from the list, but keep him/her in your waiting list. If your prospect is finding a fault in your product or service from the beginning, maybe he or she is not the right customer with whom you have to spend more time. Keep such prospects in a secondary list. When your pipeline is weak, you can take this secondary list and start following up.

Values Results & Benefits of Your Product/Service

You could have come across some customers, who will never value your product or service. When I was running a recruitment firm, some of my prospects used to say that, just by sending a resume we were making money. They don't know the difficulty in finding the right person at the right price at the right time and the risk associated with it. And they are not even ready to listen to it. If your prospect never respects or values the benefits of your service or product, then most probably he or she is going to be a very tough customer for you. He/she will keep finding fault in everything you do. If you have enough in your funnel, put such customers in the secondary list. The right prospects are the ones who understand that you bring value to the table and appreciate it. If not appreciate at least he or she should be able to acknowledge it.

Able to Make a Buying Decision in the near Future

This is a very important criterion. If the prospect is not taking a buying decision in the near future, then you are wasting all your time and energy with a wrong prospect. This is what most sales people do and this is how they waste their time. A smart sales person will identify this at the very early stage of sales cycle. By smartly asking closure questions, you can identify this. The word near future is different for different people. For some, it may be a week and for some even 3 months is a near future. Based on the value and complexity of your product/service, you have to define what is near future. The idea is, you should spend more time with somebody who will take a decision at a reasonable time period.

Good Source of Future Sales and Referrals

This is another important criterion. Sometimes, you have to work with a company because of its brand value. Even if the prospect is weak on other parameters, just for brand recall you should consider him or her as a good prospect and do diligent follow up. Imagine your prospects are from Apple, Google, or Walmart. Working with them will give you an edge on any proposal you make to other clients. Also you have to think whether this client can give you continuous business for next few years and a great source of referrals for other clients. Sometimes it may be a business group, and working with one company of that business group may give you entry to other business entities of the same business group.

If out of the above 5 parameters for a good prospect, 3 or more than 3 is positive, then you should diligently follow up with that prospect. He may be a right prospect for you. Others can be put in a secondary list and can be followed up when your pipeline is weak.

Key Takeaways:

- Top sales people spend time with right prospects
- The key is to identity the right prospect. The right prospect should have money and authority to buy

- The qualities of a good prospect are:
    - Prospect has a genuine need that your product or service can fulfil
    - Prospect is friendly toward you and has a favorable impression of you and your company
    - Prospect understands and values the results/benefits of your products/service than the amount you charge
    - Prospect is willing and will be able to make a buying decision in the near future
    - Prospect is a good source of future sales and referrals

QUESTIONING

Vidya is a Senior Sales Manager of a seven star hotel. The Program Head of one of the biggest event management companies is meeting her today. They are going to conduct one of the biggest workshops that is going to happen in the country with 5,000 plus participants. Vidya knows that she has to ask the right questions to the customer so that she can understand their needs properly and provide a solution which will clinch her the deal. But she is not sure of what kind of questions she should ask and the right sequence to ask.

The most important thing any sales person must do is questioning. Only by asking questions, you can understand the need of the customer. In order to improve your skills in questioning, I recommend the book *Spin Spelling* by Neil Rackham. It's an amazing book that elaborates about the questioning process. In this chapter, we will discuss basic questioning techniques.

Level 1 Questions

Imagine you are a sales person who is selling bottled water. You are now meeting the Head of Procurement of a five star hotel chain. During your meeting, if you ask how many bottles of water he needs, he may tell 5,000 or 10,000 bottles to solve his current need. A smart sales person will not stop there and will take it to the next level as explained below.

Sales Person: Good Morning, Sir. I am Krishna, Sales Manager of XYZ Aqua Solutions. Congratulations for your recent expansion. Would you please elaborate further on your expansion plans?

Customer: Thanks, Krishna. Yes, from 3 hotels in Bangalore, we are expanding to 7 hotels across South India.

Sales Person: That's great. And will each hotel have 200 rooms each?

Customer: Yes. That's correct. There will be anywhere between 175 to 250 rooms each.

(Back of the mind, Krishna is calculating, at 200 rooms per hotel, with 7 hotels it's 1,400 rooms. With 60% occupancy as average, it is 840 rooms per day. Assuming, the guest consumes 2 litres of water every day, it is 1,680 litres plus restaurant and bar which will make it to close to 2,000 litres of water per day which is 14,000 litres per week and 7,28,000 litres of bottled water per year)

Just by asking 2–3 questions, the sales person now sees a potential business of 7.2 litres of bottled water rather than 10,000 litres of bottled water which is an immediate need.

So, level 1 questions are those which the customer is happy and proud to share. At the same time, the questions will help the sales person to calculate the potential annual sales opportunity with that client. The kind of business conversation we will have for 7.2 lakhs litres of water business and 10,000 litres of water business will be very different. Also, we should not ask questions which are already available in the website of the company or in social media. Ask about expansion plans, growth for the current year, recruitment plans for the year etc, which will give you a good idea about the company. You can calculate your potential business accordingly.

Level 2 Questions

Once you got the answers for basic level 1 questions, which gives you the fair idea about their growth plan, now you should ask questions which will identify their needs. Needs can be either to solve their problems or to achieve their goals.

Imagine the hotel customers are keen on quality of water they consume. Currently, customers are not happy about the brand and quality of the water which is supplied. Then, it's a great opportunity for the sales guy to position his brand. He can understand this by asking the right questions on who the typical type of customers the hotel is hosting are and what the complaints generally are.

If there is no problem, then attack the GOAL the hotel wants to achieve. Ask them what type of customers they want to host. If the hotel management says they want to host a lot of business conferences and seminars, then ask the hotel what kind of water those type of customers would prefer. Keep asking questions. Get the answers from your customers. They will tell you everything you need to know.

Any business is run either to help their customers achieve their goal or to solve their customer problem. In level 2 questioning, the job of the sales person is to find out the GOAL of the customer or what problems they are trying to solve.

Level 3 Questions

Now, the sales person knows the potential business and all the basic info he needs about the customer. Now, in level 3 questioning, he has to make the customer feel what will happen if those needs are not met. If that particular problem is not solved, what will happen to his business or if the particular goal is not achieved, what are the consequences the business has to face?

Say for example, the sales person can ask the hotel management what would happen if business customers gave bad reviews online about the quality of water used in this hotel. How will those online reviews affect the occupancy rate? How much time and effort will it take them to regain the brand name? If their goal of attracting business travelers is not met, what will be the impact on the revenue and bottom line of the hotel? If you ask these kind of questions, the hotel management will think and understand the importance of not meeting their goal or not solving their problem. The job of the sales person is to ask the right questions to his customer and extrapolate it further by asking questions on what will happen to him if his needs are not met.

Level 3 questions are possible only if you are able to get the answers for your level 1 and level 2 questions. It has to go in a sequence. Directly jumping to level 3 questions will not be very effective.

Level 4 Questions

Till now, you are only asking questions. You understood the potential business, you understood his needs, and you also made him think about what would happen if his needs are not met. Now, you should present your solution. In level 4 questions, you are asking his permission to present your solution. After getting his approval, you present your solution. If your product or service will not solve his problem or will not help the customer achieve his goal, then you should not propose your solution. Then he is not your customer. But, in most cases, you will clearly be able to position your product or service as a right solution because you know what your customer problem is.

Also now he is in a position to listen to you, as you already made him to think about the consequence. Present your solution clearly, showing how it is going to benefit him in a big way. This is the time you have to talk.

All these 4 types of questioning will help the sales person to close the sale. With continuous practice, you can master the art of right questioning.

Key Takeaways:

- Top sales people will always ask right questions in a particular sequence

- Level 1 questions will help you get the basic data and will also give you an idea of potential business

- Level 2 questions will help you understand the need of the customer. The need may be to solve a particular problem or achieve a GOAL

- Level 3 questions will make the customer to think on what will happen if his needs are not met. What business consequence will he have to face?

- Level 4 questions will be to get his permission to present your solution to him

PROPOSAL WRITING

Ramesh Babu is running Solocubes, which is a Business Center. It gives a private ambience for solopreneurs and small companies. He recently got an enquiry from a Netherlands-based business consulting company, asking him to send a detailed proposal about his offerings.. His regular customers walk in to his business center and enquire about workstations. Ramesh Babu wants to write a professional business proposal which will help him win this deal.

As a sales person, you have to write a good proposal for your project. And good proposals make a difference. They portray you as a professional. In this chapter, let's understand how to write a good proposal.

Cover Page

Cover page will be the first page of the proposal. Here you should write the title of the proposal. If you are an e-learning company, use the title **"Proposal for**

Developing E-learning Content." The title should clearly communicate what this proposal is for. In the bottom of the page, write **"Submitted By"** and add your company name, logo and date.

Confidentiality Disclaimer

The second page should have Confidentiality Disclaimer. Generally the text will be like this:

This material contained in our response and any material or information disclosed during discussions of the proposal represents the proprietary, confidential information pertaining to **"your Company Name"**, services, methodologies and methods. Other products and brand names may be trademarks or registered trademarks of their respective owners.

By accepting this response, **"Client Name" agrees** that the information in this response will not be disclosed outside the organization and will not be duplicated, used, or disclosed for any purpose other than to evaluate this proposal. This proposal is subject to a mutually approved agreement or a contract specifying full terms and conditions.

The contents of this document are provided to **"Client Name" (referred as Client) in** confidence solely for the purpose of evaluating whether the contract should be awarded to **"your company name."**

Do add **"For any queries on this proposal, please contact"** and below provide your name, address, mobile number and email id.

Here is the format of the proposal.

Introduction

In Introduction, you will talk about the meeting which took place between you and the client, place and date and based on which you are submitting this proposal.

Scope

In Scope, you will explain at a macro level what this proposal is all about. Wherever possible, give numbers and timelines. Say, for example you are into website creation. Clearly mention that this project scope is to create a responsive website with so and so details. Your explanation should be under the **"What" part.**

Approach

In this section, you will be talking about the approach you are going to follow. What are the initial inputs clients have to give? How will you proceed etc. Your explanation should be under the **"How" part.**

Scope In

Now, you are explaining the scope of the project in detail. What all will be covered as part of the project? This is very important as this will be the guiding force when any dispute or problem arises in the future. So, be clear and simple in this section. It has to be clearly communicated by means of bullet points. It should capture everything you are going to do as part of this project.

Scope Out

In Scope Out, clearly communicate what you will not do as part of this project. If you don't have this section, then the client will assume a lot of things. So, be very careful and clear on what you are writing in scope out. If you have any doubts on what you can deliver, put in scope out, so that the client will come back to you if he has any doubts on this section. Here you are detailing on **What,** but at a very detailed level.

Deliverables

In this section, you have to clearly communicate what your final deliverable is. If you are branding for a company, your deliverables will be editable copy of logo, brochure, envelope design, etc. What you mention in this section is the final output your client will be expecting from you.

Timeline

In this section, talk about the timelines. Clearly mention when phase 1 will be completed and when the final phase will be completed. If you are dependent on certain information from the client and if it will affect your time line, please mention about that clearly. This section should mention about how much impact there would be on the final output for every delay of information.

Assumptions

In this section, communicate all the assumptions you are making. Also explain that you have to receive a Purchase Order before starting the project. Explain that any outstation travel cost has to be borne by the client. Whatever foreseeable assumptions you can think of, clearly communicate them here. This is to protect you from any future cost escalations.

Acceptance Criteria

In this section, explain what the acceptance criteria is. Say for example, the client will approve all your design work and then the final output is approved by email.

Any changes after that will have extra cost components etc. This section has to explain how the final outputs are approved by the client. Once approved, your work is done. Any further work will be considered as Change Request and has to be charged separately.

Pricing

In this section, explain the pricing. For single units how much is the price, for 100 units how much is the price, if you have various phases of the project, mention the price for each phase etc. Clearly indicate GST and other taxes will be extra. Indicate the price both in numbers and also in words. Pricing should not be complex; it has to be easily understood even by a kid.

Commercial Terms

In this section, explain what your payment terms are - how much is the advance? After each milestone, how much percentage has to be paid? When will you raise the invoice and after you raise the invoice within how many days payment has to be made. If the payment is not made within the agreed time frame, what will be the interest for the payment? All these information has to be presented in this section.

Validity

In this section, communicate how many days this proposal is valid for. It can be valid for one week or 15 days only. After that, a new proposal has to be made as things would have changed by then.

Key Takeaways:

A proposal should have the following sections:

- Cover Page
- Confidentiality Disclaimer
- Introduction
- Scope
- Approach
- Scope In
- Scope Out
- Deliverables
- Timeline
- Assumptions
- Acceptance Criteria
- Pricing
- Commercial Terms
- Validity

PRICING FOR PROFIT

Ilangkumaran runs an ERP implementation company. He recently sent a proposal to a cement manufacturing company for ERP implementation. He got the feedback from the client that the pricing was very high and they asked him to rework on the pricing. Ilangkumaran was not sure of whether he has to reduce the price or not.

Most entrepreneurs struggle in pricing. Many entrepreneurs are very good in their functional or technical skills. Due to fear of losing a project, they reduce the pricing and finally they end up doing the work with no profit at all. So, how do you arrive at pricing? People think you have to price a product like this:

Cost + Profit Margin = Price

Some people say,

Cost + Overheads + Profit Margin = Price

Are the above equations wrong? No, it's not wrong. But there is a better way to price. How do highly profitable companies price? We all know that Apple takes 94% profit of all the global smartphone sales. The remaining 6% is shared by 1000s of other companies. How does Apple fix its price?

In my opinion, price is the perceived value by the customer and the ability of the customer to pay that price.

Price = Perceived value by the customer and the ability of the customer to pay

We all know that a branded 1 litre water bottle costs around INR 20 in India. We can also understand that the cost of making that water will be around 1 or 2 rupees (approximately). Even that water bottle is priced very differently in different places. In a normal shop, it is INR 20. If you go to a 5 star hotel, it is INR 150. Imagine you are in a boat and the boat developed a technical fault. You are in the sea for 3 days and obviously you didn't get any water to drink. In that scenario, if I give you a bottle of branded water how much will you be willing to pay? You will be ready to pay in lakhs, right?

So, what we should understand is, price is determined by various factors. We should be open to price differently depending on the situation, location and the need of the customer. Don't sell the same product or service at the same price. Price depends upon the customer and it is not dependent on the provider. That is the key message.

You may say that in this free world, everybody knows the price of the similar product or service. Then how can I price my product or service at a premium? I agree with your point. You have to decide how to position your product or service. Do you want to position it as a low cost product or do you want to position it as a premium product? Do you want to have multiple variants of the same product or service with different price bands? It all depends upon your strategy.

For example, you get Leadership Trainers at INR 10,000 per day and also at INR 5,00,000 per day. Same is the case of a lawyer, doctor or a chartered accountant. If you have world class ability, you can charge a premium. Apple is able to charge a premium because it has developed a world class product.

So, the question now is how to charge more price to your product or service? Let me give you an example.

Imagine you are buying a Pani Poori (Indian snack usually sold on a road side) from a roadside vendor. In 2018, it costs you approximately INR 20. The same Pani Poori in a nearby restaurant costs around INR 60. The customer assumes it is worth INR 60, three times more than the road side vendor. Which Pani Poori will be tasty? In most cases, it will be the road side Pani Poori which is tastier.

So, how is the restaurant able to charge 3 times more for the same ingredients? Because he/she is adding value by giving a nice ambience, a better place to sit and have it and by projecting they are very hygienic. For all the above additional value, the cost per Pani Poori will be around INR 5. By adding value worth INR 5, they are able to charge INR 35 more (20 + 5 = 25 and 60 − 25 = 35).

Now, as entrepreneurs and as sales executives, we have to think, how by adding a marginal extra cost, we can add more value and price our product/service 2 times, 3 times, 5 times more than the market price.

Also please note that for some customers, if you price it cheap you are going to lose the deal. Imagine a customer who is coming in an Audi Car and he is asking how much would you charge for a business profile photo shoot (Assume you are a photographer).

If you say INR 10,000, you will lose the deal. The customer is not ready to have his business profile photo shoot with someone with whom anybody can have a profile shoot. You should charge him INR 1,00,000 and you have to think how you can give value and justification for your price. At the end of the day, the customer should feel that he has got more value than for what he paid.

Sometimes, there will be a situation, where you don't have time to profile the customer. He meets you in a lift, asks about your service and without giving much details asks you for a price. In that scenario, what should you do? If you are not very sure of how to price, then the best thing is to ask him, " How much are you willing to pay?" He may give you some number. The moment somebody gives you a number, then it means he is ready to pay little more than that. In the above example, say if the person who came in an Audi car says, "I am willing to pay INR 50,000." Then in reality, he is willing to pay INR 60K or INR 70K. Then you can quote 75K and close it anywhere between 50K to 75K.

We will see one more example. In MG Road, Bangalore, India, in all the traffic signals you have to wait for 60 to 90 seconds. There will be many sellers who will quickly come near the car and sell you cooling glass, toys, mobile cover etc. One such day, my friend and I were in a car and were waiting at a signal. My friend is a very good negotiator. Suddenly one fellow came with a very beautiful Vinayaka statue made out of plaster of paris. He quoted INR 1,200. My friend liked the statue and he asked him how much he could give it for. (Remember, my friend didn't give any number), then immediately the seller told he can give it for INR 800. (From 1,200 suddenly he came to 800). My friend told him it was not worth more than INR 200, and if the seller was ready to give for this price, he would take it. The traffic signal showed 15 seconds. The seller then reduced the price to INR 500 and my friend took INR 300 from his pocket and told the seller if he could give it for INR 300, he would take it and finally he got it for INR 300.

Do you think the seller would have made a loss by selling it for INR 300? Definitely not. He still would have made a good profit. But see how much he started the price with. He decided the price by seeing the car you are travelling. My friend was driving a Suzuki Baleno. If it's an Audi, he would have started with a different price. My friend was smart enough to negotiate. But I know many people who bought the same Vinayaka statue for INR 1,000.

The point I want to communicate here is don't be rigid with your price. Be flexible. Based on your customer, their need, timing and place, price it accordingly. Pricing for profit is more important than just pricing.

Whenever we price a product or service, we should always come up with two prices. **Quoted Price and Walkaway Price**. Say for example, if you have a project, where your cost comes to INR 5,000, then in general we quote INR 6,000 with 20% margin. But we never think about unknown risks and unforeseen challenges. Also we never give any buffer for negotiation, because we always negotiate with ourselves in our mind.

So, I recommend if your cost comes to INR 5,000 and your intuition says that the customer's perceived value is INR 7,000, then you should quote INR 10,000. I said you should quote INR 10,000; that doesn't mean that your final price is INR 10,000. Obviously the customer is going to come back and negotiate with you. Whatever price you quote, he is going to negotiate with you. Have enough buffer for negotiation and enough buffer for future unforeseen challenges. Now, you can close the deal anywhere between INR 7,000 to INR 10,000. I would even recommend, have a clear walk away price. In this case, it can be either INR 6,000 or INR 7,000. Walk away price is the price below which you will not take the deal. Once you have a clear understanding of the quoted price and walk away price, then you can always win deals with profits.

Let me give one more example. When I was running an e-learning company, we had to quote for a project. The project had multiple files and the quote had to be for each file. We had to deliver 1000s of such files. My delivery team came up with the costing. Each file would cost us INR 500 and if we got the deal at INR 600, we would be profitable. I quoted INR 1,200 and finally closed the deal at INR 1,000. As expected, there were project overruns and we ended up incurring a cost of INR 600 per file. Also when the project was over, the customer came to us and told that they ended up in a big loss and asked us to reduce the price by 10% so that they can make the payment. Even though it is not fair for them to ask like this, we accepted this request. Finally, we reduced the price by 10% on our invoice and raised the invoice at INR 900. We lost 10% in our costing and we lost 10% during our invoice stage. Still we made INR 300 profit per file because we priced it better. These are the real life problems we will face. Even after completing our work, clients may still ask us to reduce price. Hence it is always better to have a walkaway price which will withstand all these unforeseen price fluctuations.

Key Takeaways:

- Cost + Overheads + Profit Margin should not be your price
- Price = perceived value by the customer and the ability of the customer to pay
- Price depends upon the customer and it is not dependent on the product/service provider
- At the end of the day, the customer should feel that he has got more value than for what he paid
- By spending little extra, we can add more value to our product/service and price it 2 times, 3 times, 5 times more than the market price
- Don't be rigid with your price. Be flexible. Based on your customer, their need, the timing and the place, price it accordingly
- Whenever you price a product or service, you should always come up with 2 prices: **Quoted Price and Walkaway Price**
- Never negotiate with yourselves. Negotiation should happen only with the customer
- Once you have a clear understanding of quoted price and walk away price, then you can always win deals with profits

RESPONSE TIME AS COMPETITIVE STRATEGY

Smart sales people use response time as a competitive strategy. Here are a few questions to think.

1. When you are talking to a prospect for the first time over phone, and if they ask you when could you meet, what would your answer be?
2. After a face-to-face meeting with your customer, when do you send your minutes of meeting mail?
3. When a customer asks you when you would send your proposal, what would your answer be?

Whenever a prospective customer talks to you over phone and asks you "when can we meet," my suggestion to you is tell them that you can meet them today. The customer will most probably say that he is busy and would prefer to meet you tomorrow or day after. But he/she would definitely be impressed that you are willing to meet them the same day.

You may have a question in mind, "How can you go for a meeting immediately when your calendar is already full for the day?" If you have any other important meeting which you cannot cancel, then you should ask the customer for a meeting tomorrow. If you are free, or you have a meeting which is internal, or any other meeting which is not of great importance, then you postpone that meeting and attend this customer who is talking to you for the first time. It makes a huge positive first impression.

Whenever I talk to such prospects for the first time, and when they ask me when can we meet, I ask them where their office is. If they say Koramangala (a place in Bangalore, India) which is an one hour travel from my office, I will inform the customer that I can meet him in 90 minutes from now. Generally, they don't get such a response and it will create a positive first impression.

One of my good friends who is a successful sales person used to send minutes of meeting within 15 minutes of the meeting. After the meeting with the customer, he would sit in the reception, open his laptop and send the minutes immediately. If there was any action pending from his side, he would mention that in the mail and commit a time frame and say, within 24 hours he would update on this particular item and also put the action items on the customer side in the mail. But always, within 15 minutes of the meeting with the customer, he would send the minutes of the meeting mail. For the past 3 years, he has been the recipient of the Best Salesman award in his company.

In general, we all believe that when an action item is pending, it is better to complete that and then send the mail. Don't make the customer to wait till then. Acknowledge them that you are working on the action item. In the worst case scenario, your minutes of the meeting mail should reach the customer within 24 hours of the meeting. The best sales people do it in 15 minutes.

When a customer is asking you to send a proposal, how much time do you take to send it? Many of my vendors send me a proposal after 3 days, and some send after 5 days. I lose interest with them. Smart sales people always send the proposal within 24 hours. They would have created a proposal template already and only those details which are specific to this client have to be edited and they come up with a pricing and send the proposal the same day or the next day. This shows that the sales guy is very much interested in the business and he acts fast. Only 3–4 major things he has to change in the proposal: Customer name, scope in, approach (mostly it will be common) and the price. Rest all can be a template in a word doc which can be quickly used. When I was a customer, I didn't like my vendor partners who would send their proposal in 5 days or one week.

> You want to paint your house which you bought 5 years back. The wall paints are faded and you want to give a fresh look. You have to post an online classified and 5 painters have called you. You ask the same question to all 5 of them, asking when they can visit your house and have a discussion. Out of the 5, one guy called Satish asked you where your house was and based on the distance he was at your house within next 30 minutes. And when he reached your house, he had all the tools to measure the size and after discussion and measurement, he gave you the proposal instantly and when you asked him when he could start the work, he said within 48 hours he would start the work.

And let's assume Satish quoted INR 20,000 for the painting work. His entire interaction gets over within 1 hour. He came, did the inspection, gave the quote and was ready with a date to start the work.

On the other hand, imagine the other painters met you after 1 or 2 days, gave the quote after 2 days from your meeting and are interested to start the work after 5 days from the date of quote. Their price is in the range of INR 16,000 to INR 20,000 – whom do you choose?

Think for a minute. Most of us will choose Satish whose response time is very fast. We all would be thoroughly impressed by him. To win this deal, did he price less? Did he give any offer? Actually he is a little premium. But still we all liked him. That's the message we have to learn. Response time is a competitive strategy. If you do all the things right and fast, you can delight the customer. You can win deals. It doesn't need any extra cost, or extra effort and only needs attitude change and discipline.

During any sales stage, if a customer is calling you and asking you about any reference or any other small info and asks you when you can give it to them, answer that you will send it to them in 30 seconds. Yes, I said 30 seconds. And after the call, send it in 30 seconds. Remember when you say seconds, even if it is delayed, the delay will be in seconds, if you say minutes, delay will also be in minutes. I know people will laugh at you when you initially say this because they are not used to it. They laugh at you initially, then they think about you, then they admire you and then they follow you. You can see that their language also changes. This is the pattern. I have personally experienced it.

I know entrepreneurs who use response time as their competitive strategy and win more deals. But only very few people are able to do this as it requires a disciplined approach to everything you do. Your planning on resource and on equipment (if you need any) should fall in place to commit and react at such a pace. In other words, all your solution teams, your delivery teams, and your resource planning teams should be aligned to this attitude. Faster response time should be your company's way of life.

Key Takeaways:

- Whenever a prospective customer asks you for a face-to-face meeting, meet him the same day

- Minutes of the meeting mail should go within 24 hours of the meeting. Great sales people do it in 15 minutes

- Have a proposal template created and ready always. Periodically update the template

- Send the proposal within 24 hours from the time customer asks for it

- Make faster response time as the attitude of your company

- Align all the divisions in the company to this attitude

CROSS SELLING AND UP SELLING

Rajeev Kumar runs a financial consulting services company called Profin. Many of his clients approach him for advice on getting loans from banks. Rajeev knows that the same customers can use his service for adopting a better financial strategy or for advice on project finance etc. Rajeev wants to sell his other services to his existing clients.

We have seen many sales gurus talking about cross selling and up selling. What is it all about? As an entrepreneur and a sales person, what is this to you? We have been to McDonalds many times. You can see the person in the counter asking "Can I add fries to it?" or "Sir, Can I make it a meal?" It is nothing but cross selling!

Cross selling is the art of suggesting additional, complementary items to someone who has already decided on a purchase.

Imagine you are buying a suit. After deciding which suit to buy, the sales person will ask you whether he can show you some tie which will match the suit color. You will most probably say yes to it. Please observe the timing in this situation. The salesperson usually asks you this question only after you made the buying decision for your suit. Now think about the products or services you can cross sell to your customer. If you are selling computers or laptops, you can think about selling printers, Bluetooth speakers etc. You should definitely have a list of items ready to cross sell.

So, why is cross selling important? When the customer has already made a buying decision, he is in a favorable mindset with the product or service you are offering. At this point in time, it is easy to sell him another product or service which will add value to him. Here, as a seller you should not be greedy. The thumb rule is, the product or service you are cross selling should not exceed 10 to 20% of the product or service the customer is purchasing in the first place. Say the customer is buying a suit for INR 10,000, you can sell a tie worth anywhere between INR 1,000 to INR 2,000. It's not a fixed rule, but if you become greedy, then the customer will not buy your idea.

What is up selling? *It is the practice of encouraging customers to purchase a comparable higher-end product than the one in question.*

Ten years back, I decided to buy my first car. My budget was around INR 3,00,000. I went to a Maruthi Suzuki showroom along with my wife. The sales person in the showroom was cordial. He asked us a lot of questions like how many members are there in my family, whether we go for a long drive etc. He also asked about the distance between my office and home, how many kids I have, if there are elders staying with us, etc. Then he showed us a Maruthi Swift car which had a on road price of INR 4,80,000. When I told him I was not looking for a Swift model and preferred a small car, he told us that, it's ok if I didn't buy it, and that he just wanted me to experience it to check if it suits my needs.

Then me and my wife sat in that car and he started to explain the various features of the car and why it would be a perfect fit for our family and our needs. Finally, my wife was so convinced to buy that car and I had no choice and ended up buying that car which was way above my budget at that time. This is an excellent example of up selling. If you want to truly upsell, you should ask all the right questions to the customer and make him feel the experience of the product or service you are upselling.

> Senthil Pandian works as a sales person in a retail mobile store. Once a middle-aged man came to the store and told him that he needed a smart phone. Senthil Pandian asked the customer the reasons for buying this smartphone. Is it to upgrade from the existing phone or to gift it to anybody? The customer replied that he wanted to give this phone as a gift. Senthil Pandian asked him who he was gifting it to and what the occasion for gifting was.
>
> The customer told that he wanted to gift it to his mother as she was turning 60 years. Then Senthil Pandian asked him, "I am sure your mother would have taken good care of you and you want to give her the best phone. Tell me your budget." The customer told him that he initially had a budget of INR 10,000 but he was okay to pay little more if the phone is good.
>
> Senthil Pandian showed the customer how his mother would be more comfortable in using an iphone as it is user friendly and comes with a good camera. Finally, he sold iphone 6 to the customer for INR 30,000. This is up selling. He made an upsell of INR 20,000. When you ask right questions to the customers and connect with them emotionally, they will be ready to spend more than their initial budget.

Key Takeaways:

- Always have a list of product/service ready for cross selling

- Don't be greedy. The product/service you are cross selling should not exceed 20% of the value of the primary product you are selling in the first place

- If you want to upsell, first ask all the right relevant questions

- Make the customer feel the experience of the product you are going to upsell

NEGOTIATION

Ezhil is a commercial architect. She submits a proposal to design commercial projects. Based on her proposal, she is called for meetings to negotiate on price. She knows that her designs are very good and customers also like it. She feels by mastering the art of negotiation she can win more deals.

Negotiation is a skill which every sales person should master. If you want to be a good sales person, then you have to be good in negotiation. Negotiation in itself is a big subject which needs to be explained in a separate book. I recommend Author William Ury's *Getting to Yes* and *Negotiation Genius* by Deepak Malhotra and Max Bazerman.

In any negotiation for that matter, we should never try to win everything for ourselves. Especially in sales, where relationship matters a lot, you should always think about the other party as well and work toward the most acceptable outcome for both sides. It is important to understand why negotiation fails and how to avoid it during your sales cycle.

Ego

One of the main reasons why negotiation fails is ego. After a certain point, both parties take it personally and want to win at any way. If you are a sales person ready to accept your mistakes or adjust even if you are not wrong, then it will pave way for win-win outcomes. Many a time, as a sales person when the prospective customer doesn't communicate properly or acknowledge your communication, it will make you feel bad about yourself. Self-ego comes into picture, and you will think, if the customer wants your product/service, let them come back, and you are not going to call them again. May be the prospective customer would have forgotten or got into many other things. He/she may be waiting for your call for negotiation on the price or terms so that you can make a deal. So, when you are a sales person, during negotiation forget your ego and focus only on the subject of negotiation.

Fear

Fear is another important reason why negotiation fails. When you desperately want to come to an agreement because you cannot afford to lose this customer, then you will agree to anything the prospective customer asks for. So even if there is an agreement based on the outcome and you are not happy, this means it's a failure. Fear comes when there is lack of options, sometimes due to lack of knowledge and sometimes due to lack of preparation. So, before negotiating, have a clear back up plan and also have thorough knowledge about the customers' business so that you can understand why he is asking about what he is asking.

Rigidity

During negotiation, if you are too rigid and want to win everything, then negotiation will most likely fail. You should be flexible to accommodate some of the requests made by the other party. Only then, can we reach win-win outcomes. Rigidity kills negotiation.

Lack of Preparation

This is the most important reason for negotiation failures. Before going for a negotiation, prepare your 4W and 1H questions.

- What do I want from this negotiation?

- Why do I want this from my prospective customer?
- Who has to take part from my team for this negotiation?
- When do I want to get the things I want?
- How am I going to present my case?

Once you are clear on all the above 5 questions, you have to think about what the answers from the other party for the same 5 questions will be. He/she will also have the same questions for his preparation. If you are able to think of the 5 questions of your opposite party and ready to give him some of it, then you have high chances of win-win outcomes.

Another best way to prepare is have your **BATNA – Best Alternative To a Negotiated Agreement** in place. Before going into any negotiation, you should have a backup plan ready. Then you can accept anything which is better than your BATNA.

I was selling my used Swift car 2 years back. As soon as I put my advertisement in an online classified, one buyer called me and offered to take the car for INR 2.7 lakhs. I told him that I would get back to him by the next day. Then when the next buyer called me and visited my house to inspect the car, I was very confident and negotiated with him for a price of INR 2.8 lakhs, because I have a BATNA of INR 2.7 lakhs. It may not be very easy to have a BATNA when you are dealing with your customer for your projects, but with careful thinking and execution, you can have a clear BATNA so that you can negotiate better.

Similarly, when a customer is calling you for a negotiation where you have to reduce your price or increase the payment terms (which is also a part of sales person's job), be ready to have your **WATNA – Worst Alternative To a Negotiated Agreement.** If any deal is better than the WATNA, you can accept it. If your WATNA is 90 days' payment and the offer on the table is 60 days, then it is better to accept the deal which is better than your WATNA.

Emotional

Another important reason why negotiation fails is because of emotions. It can be getting emotional about your product/service or getting emotional about your company. Sometimes, prospective customers make you emotional and leverage your emotions to get a better deal. Emotions can be making you angry, sympathetic or happy etc. They may ask you to reduce the price, saying that the final output is going for a good cause and they will ask you not to negotiate on it. If as an entrepreneur or sales person you want to do something for a good cause, then you do it in your personal capacity, you don't have to do it during a negotiation. We should know how to detach our emotions during a negotiation. Also people will make unnecessary complaints about your product/service and make you feel either angry or guilty and leverage that in the negotiation. Don't give up in such situations.

Key Takeaways:

- Negotiation is very important for all sales people. You have to master it as a sales person

- Ego, fear, rigidity, lack of preparation, emotions etc. are all reasons for negotiation failure

- During negotiation, think about the needs of the other party as well so that you can work toward win-win outcomes

- Preparing your BATNA and WATNA before the negotiation will help you reach an agreement

OBJECTION HANDLING

Ramesh is a sales executive working in a company which sells batteries and UPS. He has a target to meet every month. He is a hard working person, but every time he meets a client, he faces different objections. Some say his products are very costly, others say they already have a vendor and they don't have a need to talk to a new supplier. A few others collect all details from him and just say they will get back to him when there is a need.

Almost all sales people face these type of situations every day. How do you handle such objections? Do we have a way to handle these objections? Typically, objections fall under any of these 4 categories:

1. Objections due to price and budget
2. Objections about competition

3. Objections about need and fit
4. Objections about authority to buy

In general, smart sales people handle objections using LAER model. LAER stands for **L**isten, **A**cknowledge, **E**xplore and **R**espond. When a customer raises an objection, actively listen to it. Don't try to answer. Once he completes, acknowledge that you understood his point of view. Explore more on the objection, ask questions if needed and get more information. Once you clearly understood and have all the data, then you can respond to the objection.

Objections Due to Price & Budget

Objection	Response
It's too expensive	Talk about value of your service rather than price
There is no money	Maybe really your prospect doesn't have money. Track him for future business. When your business expands, approach him again. Currently, he may not be your right customer

| We don't have budget | Think innovatively and come out with different pricing options. May be you can ask them for small EMIs and as they grow, they can increase the monthly payout |

Indhu is into communication and behavioral training. Whenever she meets a new prospective client, their typical response is that they already have a behavioral trainer as their partner. Many of you will be in a similar situation. Objections due to competition is very common. How do you handle this?

Objections Due to Competition

Objection	Response
I am already working with Company ABC	It is actually positive for you. You don't need to educate them about your product or service. Ask the prospective customer what is working very well with the existing vendor and what is not working. You will get

	some complaints. Address those complaints and explain to them how your service will eliminate such issues
I am locked in a contract with company X for 18 months	Analyze whether this is a real objection. If it's true, explain to them how they will financially still benefit by signing with you for 3 years. Give them the clear cost benefit analysis. Also explain to them the benefits they will get by signing up with you
I can get a cheaper version of your product from other vendors	It may be a negotiation tactic. Talk about the value and not about the price. Give your best price and walk away. You can find enough customers who can pay your price

I am very happy with my existing vendor	Talk about de-risking. Working with one vendor has its own pitfalls. Ask them to give just 10% of existing work to diversify the risk. Then you can always penetrate for a larger pie

Subodh Pandit is a sales engineer who sells artificial intelligence based recruitment solutions. Many of his prospective customers don't understand his language. Prospective customers feel they don't have any need for the product he is selling. Subodh wants to find a solution for this problem.

Objections About Need & Fit

Objection	Response
I have never heard about your company	Treat this as request for information. Tell about your existing clients who are similar to the prospect
I don't see what your product could do for me	Again this is asking for information. Tell them

	clearly how your product or service can solve your prospects' problem
I don't understand your product	It actually happens if your product or service is little technical or complicated. Understand what part they are not clear and bring a technical guy or a product engineer to explain in detail
I don't see a potential ROI	Here you have to go with numbers in depth. Take case studies on how in the past, similar customers benefitted

Jinoo is a real estate consultant. She was talking to a prospective client who wanted to buy 10 acres of land to build a farm house. Jinoo showed him many properties which were on the outskirts of the city. After working with this prospective customer for more than 1 month showing him more than 10 properties, finally the prospective customer told her that the final decision would be taken by his father who is in the US and he would be coming to India only after 2 months. Jinoo felt bad that her 2 months of efforts were wasted.

Objections About Authority to Buy

Objection	Response
I am not authorized to sign off on this purchase	Get the right person to speak. Do this at the initial sales cycle. This can be achieved by asking right questions during the initial sales stage
I can't sell this internally within my company	Help them how to sell it internally. Work with them. Understand the objections he will face internally. Coach them. If needed, arrange for a meeting where you can go and support him

Key Takeaways:

- Objection handling is most critical for the closure of the sale

- Objections can be broadly classified into 4 categories

    o Objections due to Price and Budget

    o Objections about Competition

    o Objections about Need & Fit

    o Objections about Authority to buy

- Objections when handled effectively will be a great competitive advantage

CLOSING THE SALE

Suresh Kumar is a business consultant who advises small and medium enterprise CEOs on business strategy. He meets a lot of entrepreneurs every week. When they interact with him, they find a need to use his service for their business. Suresh Kumar sends them a proposal within next 2 days, and after that there is no response from the prospective customer. The price is also very competitive. Suresh Kumar wants to know how to proceed further. His challenge is to get closure of the sale. Many entrepreneurs and sales executives struggle on how to effectively close the deal.

When can we conclude that the deal is closed? The deal is closed once we have the advance payment received and purchase order is released. Many companies release the purchase order and advance payment together. If you are in a business where advance payment is not possible, then the agreement has to be signed by both the parties and purchase order or statement of work has to be released. Then we can conclude that the sale is closed. There are different ways of closing a sale.

Assumed Consent Close

In Assumed Consent Close, you assume that the client already made a decision and you go for closing questions.

1. Which color do you prefer – blue or green?
2. Can I deliver it by Saturday morning or Sunday morning?
3. Do you want to make the payment monthly or quarterly?
4. Can we fill the agreement now?

Above are the typical closure questions sales people ask using this technique. You can see this very often when you are buying a Saree in a textile shop in India. As a sales person, you have to always go for the closure question. ABC is very famous in sales terminology. ABC stands for Always be closing.

Ben Franklin Close

It is also called as Balance Sheet Close. Take a sheet of paper and divide it by a line vertically. One the left side, write "Pros" and help your client to write down all the positive points of buying your product or service. For example, if you are selling smart phones, give him pointers about good camera quality, long battery life etc. On the right side, ask him to write "Cons" and don't help him. Let him think and write. After completing the exercise, you can see that there will be more positive points on left and few negative points on right side. Then you can go for the closure question and close the deal. It's very effective in B2C, which is Business to Consumer sales.

Silence Close

After a closing question, remain silent but maintain eye contact. For example, after asking whether the buyer can sign the contract, the buyer will be thinking of many things in his mind. As a sales person, we lose patience after 30 seconds, then we start saying that we can reduce price by another 10%. Actually the buyer was not thinking about the price. He was thinking about how to effectively start using your product. If you keep the silence a little longer, you tend to gain more. On the other side, by keeping himself silent, the buyer makes you confused and you give in early. So, after the closure question, remain silent. This closure technique is very effective.

Pointed Close

Pointed close needs a lot of confidence and seasoned sales professionals use it very effectively. Say for example, "If this takes care of your need and falls within your budget, can we start the paper work?" "If we commit to deliver 1 ton of rice every week at the price you agreed, will you release the purchase order now?"

These are the pointed closure questions sales people ask, if they are very confident about the product or service and when they know the client very well.

Hard to Get Close

In hard to get close, you create a perception in the mind of the customer that it is very hard to get your product or service. Google used it when they launched Gmail. Those days, you could use Gmail only when somebody using Gmail referred you. One Plus one mobiles used it effectively when they entered India.

Power of Closure Questions

50% of sales conversations happen without a closure question. In the example cited at the beginning of this chapter, Suresh Kumar was struggling because of not using closure questions. Then after attending a Sales

Training workshop, he started using closure questions effectively. By asking the right closure questions, objections will come out. Suresh Kumar understood that his prospective customers had the objection of allotting specific time every week for his sessions. When he addressed that objection effectively, he was able to win more clients.

Go for closure questions like,

When will they sign the contract?

When will they release the purchase order?

When will they release the advance?

By continuously asking closure questions and effectively addressing objections, you can win more deals.

Key Takeaways:

- Closure questions bring out objections if any
- Assumed consent close assumes that the customer has already made a buying decision
- Ben Franklin close lists out pros and cons and asks the prospective customer to list them out

- Silence close is very effective; use it after asking a closure question

- Pointed close is used by experienced sales people and is used when you know the customer needs very well

- Hard to get close creates a perception of premium about your product or service

EFFECTIVE NETWORKING

Rajanikanth is a leadership trainer who runs Win and Win Leadership Academy. Every year, Rajanikanth invests 5% of his earnings on himself and attends many seminars and conferences. Whenever he attends such seminars, he meets many people and follow ups with them for any possible future business. Still Rajanikanth feels there is a better way of networking, and he wants to be very effective in networking to win more business.

Every sales person should understand and master networking. As they say, *Smart people network and others work for them.* As the word indicates, it is net "work." We have to work on it. I know many people get scared the moment they see 100 people around them. The best way to get out of this fear is to attend many seminars and conferences and get used to it.

If you go to a seminar or a conference and see 100 people and exchange cards with them, it is not networking. It's not about collecting business cards, but about building trust with right people and following it up with them periodically if you see potential business.

Always Go Early

Top networkers always go early to meetings, seminars or conferences. When you go early, you have multiple advantages. First, you can choose the best seat. Say, you can sit in the first row where you are highly visible to the speaker. Also when you go early, the people who are already there, say 3 to 5 people, they will automatically come and talk to you. They are forced to speak to you as they don't have many people in the room. Even if you are an introvert, by just following this tip you will be easily able to mingle with people. You also have a good chance of spending quality time with the key note speaker.

Ask Open-ended Questions

Many of my training participants ask me this question. What should they speak to a stranger? I have given them 5 basic questions with which they can start a conversation.

1. Which business are you into?
2. How is the business doing?
3. In the current market scenario, what are the opportunities you are foreseeing?
4. What are your current challenges?
5. Which type of customers will be useful for you so that I connect them to you?

These open-ended questions will make them speak to you. You can also genuinely help them if you have right contacts. If not help, you can at least learn something new. As you are actively listening, they will in turn ask you what you are doing and then you can talk about your business and about yourself.

Don't Sell, Build Trust

Many people try to sell when they go for a conference or a seminar. My suggestion is at a short span of time, it will be tough for you to sell. Meet people and work on building trust. You can collect cards and take notes if you find any potential opportunity for business. Get their permission on whether you can meet them the following week. If possible, send a calendar invite from your smartphone immediately. Only during that follow up meeting, you have to sell your product or service. Never try to sell at the first instance.

Be Ready with Your 60 seconds Pitch

You never know whom you are going to meet in a seminar or a conference. If they ask you to tell about your business, you should be ready. Your pitch has to be clear and specific. You have to talk about your name, your business name, the service/product you offer/create, the benefit to the customer, why you are good and a recent success story. If you tell all the above in a crisp manner, it will not exceed 60 seconds. Practice it again, again and again.

Also when people ask you, how they can help you, you have to be clear with your answers. You should be ready with what help you want. If you want any specific company connections, be ready with it. If you are ready to do a free pilot or proto type, communicate it.

Be Well Dressed

You don't know whom you are going to meet. It is always better to go with the best outfit you have. Your outfit has to suit the occasion. People love to interact with folks who are well dressed. It takes only 7 seconds to make a first impression about a person. It's definitely worth planning your attire.

Tell Stories

When you are interacting with strangers during networking, tell them short stories. Share with them the stories about your experience with customers. Your stories have to be interesting, short and should reveal the benefit your product or service given to the customer. People always remember stories. Be creative. Say for example, you had a meeting in Goa with a customer, talk something good about Goa, its culture, its food etc, along with the experience of that meeting. Remember, you are not selling your product, you are selling the benefit your product brings. Don't talk for more than 3-4 minutes. Your story has to be short; otherwise it will be boring.

Follow Up

As they say, fortune lies in follow up. Everybody forgets you within 3 days. Within first 24 hours of the seminar or conference, write down a brief mail. If they are good prospects, meet them within 3-5 days. When you are writing a mail, just write 3-5 lines, don't write big paragraphs. Your mail should create enough interest so that they give you an appointment. Follow up, follow up, follow up. That's the only way people will remember you.

Network Everywhere

People think they have to network only during big gatherings like seminars or conferences. Smart sales folks network everywhere. They talk to security people who have the right information about whether the CEO is in town or not. They network with receptionist, finance people, HR people, and procurement people. The more you build relationships, the more data you get access to. With more data, you can make the right decision. If you want to be a successful sales person, you should know how to network with all sorts of people. Good networkers are genuinely interested in people. They don't network just for the sake of benefit. When you are genuinely interested in people, they help you every time, everywhere.

Key Takeaways:

- For a seminar or a conference, always go early
- In a networking meeting, always ask open-ended questions
- Be a good listener
- Don't sell, build trust

- Be ready with your 60 seconds pitch
- Be well dressed
- Tell stories
- Follow up
- Network everywhere

HANDLING INTERNAL TEAMS

eRx Solutions is a health-tech company based in Bangalore. Being a lean start up, eRx Solutions needs to galvanize its entire team to inspire customers' confidence. Shobhit Mathur, director and co-founder of the company, does that by taking care of every member in the team. eRx invests in their team members, be it their career growth, personal well-being or acquisition of new skills to keep them relevant in the job market. Shobhit understands that handling internal teams is key to company's success.

Some times as a sales person, you need the help of your internal team member to win a deal. Say, if you are selling technology service or technology product, you need the help of solution architects or pre sales teams. How do you get the best support from them? This makes a crucial part of you winning a deal.

This is where your people skills come into picture. People work for people. People don't care about what you know until they know you care about them. So, it's very important to network within your company if you want to be a successful sales person.

Include Them in Success

Actions which are rewarded and recognized will be repeated. Whenever you get support, acknowledge their contribution. When you win a deal, announce to the entire world about the people who contributed to this win. You can be little extra in your praising. A leader is one who takes less appreciation than he deserves and takes more criticism than he deserves. The moment people know that you are acknowledging their contribution in success, they will keep working for you. Trust me, the power of your position or your fancy designation is not going to help you.

If you are an entrepreneur, the same above principles apply. But you have to do little more than that. You have to convince your co-founding team on why this deal is so important for the company and how it is going to help the future of the company apart from the cash flow it brings. Your skill as a salesperson starts first by selling your idea to your cofounding team.

Separate Them from the Failures

When deals fail, take the complete responsibility. Write a mail to everybody internally involved in the deal about you taking complete responsibility for the failure and thank them for their contribution for the great effort. This will make them work for you in the future. Also, when there is a high risk work, you tell your people that you will take the complete responsibility of the outcome. This will make them stress free and out of fear so that they can completely focus on doing the work in hand.

Celebrate Success

If you are handling a sales team, or you are a sales person and working with many other functions to complete your sales deal, do remember to celebrate every small success. Whether the deal is big or small, celebrate it with people. This will make people work for you whole heartedly for your next deal. When I say celebrate, it's not only about the food or drink or party that is motivating people, it's actually you acknowledging their contribution and spending time with them on celebration. That is the real motivation for people.

Give Visibility to your Team

If you are handling a sales team, then as head of sales it's your responsibility to give maximum visibility to your team. When I was working for a Top 10 IT Services company as a Sales Manager, my boss Paritosh Segal used to do it beautifully. For every little extra effort I put, he would give me great visibility by appreciating my work and propagating it across senior leadership. This act of him made me work more for the company and more for him. It's very important to give visibility to your team. Imagine after winning a deal, you as a Sales Leader are going to your team member's house and giving a box full of sweets to his family and thanking the family for the support, how will your team member feel? How will the family feel about your company? Next time, the family will motivate your team member to burn that midnight oil for you. Winning is all about handling your team right.

Lead from the Front

Another important factor for getting absolute support from your team is the way you are leading from the front. If during Diwali, (a big festival in India) your team member is on a tour, meeting prospective customer, and you are at home celebrating Diwali, it will not go well. Are you joining him, sacrificing your Diwali celebration? Even though your presence is not needed for that deal, if you are able to do it, people will work for you. Maybe your team member will say, you are not needed now and you can go and celebrate Diwali. The kind of caring you give to your people is what is going to decide whether you are going to be a successful sales person or not.

Key Takeaways:

- Handling internal teams effectively is key to sales success
- Include your team in all your successes
- Separate them in all the failures and you take complete responsibility
- Wherever possible, give visibility to the team which worked for you
- Lead from the front. Be there for your team whenever they need you

FOLLOW UP

Gomathi Ramesh is the founder of an e-learning company. She has a strong lead generation engine. and is a member of many networking associations and through them she gets good leads. But her sales team is not able to convert the leads into business. After a lot of analysis, she found that lack of proper follow up was the main reason for the failure.

As a sales person or as an entrepreneur, how many times do we follow up? One time, 2 times, after that we get a feeling that we don't want to follow up again. If the customer wants your service or product, let them call. After all, you are giving a great service, then why should you call them when they don't pick your call?

This little voice is in the mind of many entrepreneurs and sales people. Author Jack Canfield, in his book *Success Principles* has written:

"Herbert True, a marketing specialist at Notre Dame University, found that

44% of all sales people quit trying after the first call

24% quit after the second call

14% quit after the third call

12% quit after the fourth call"

Now, let's go deep into this statistics. What it means is, 44% of people don't follow up after first call. 94% people don't follow up after 4th call. Just by following for the 5th time, you are eliminating 94% of your competitors. By making that 5th call, your competition is irrelevant to you. Great competitive advantage. The other statistics say that worldwide, across all business, 60% deals are closed only after the 4th call.

If you see both the statistics together, we understand that only 6% of sales people or entrepreneurs win 60% of worldwide business. For the remaining 40% business, those 94% of people who follow up to 4 times and this 6% people who follow up more than 4 times both compete.

Sundar is running a translation services company. One day, he got connected to a funded company in education space. He spoke to the CEO of that company and the CEO introduced him to the COO. He had a great meeting with that COO, and after that he started following up with the COO through mail, marking the CEO in copy.

After 5 follow ups, one day the COO informed Sundar that he was irritated with continuous mails and informed him that he was also taking his CEO's time by marking him in the mail and asked him to stop follow up. Did Sundar stop following up? No, after 10 days he again started following up, and finally he ended up doing business worth more than INR10 million with them. When I asked Sundar why he didn't stop following up after he was explicitly told to stop, Sundar replied that he would take it as that on that particular day COO was in a bad mood and he would have just had a fight with someone, got irritated and would have seen his mail and replied to him like that. So he didn't take that mail seriously. No business person will get irritated by follow up. We all know that fortune lies in follow up. This is a very positive way of looking at things, which shows the importance of diligent follow up.

Many of Sundar's customers told him that they gave him business because they liked the way he followed up with them. So is there a way to follow up?

When to follow up? Which day is the right day? Which time is the right time? How many times can we do follow up? Will the customer be irritated if we follow up too much? These are the questions we all have in our mind.

Actually it depends upon the customer. When I was running my recruitment business a few years back, I was trying to reach one of my customers. Whenever I called her, she would never pick my phone. I used to call her in morning, afternoon, and evening. She would always send me a message saying she was busy. One Saturday, I thought of calling her on a weekend to see whether she would pick my call. To my surprise, she picked my call on the first ring, and spoke to me for one hour. At the end of the call, I openly asked her why she was not picking my calls on week days and how she was able to give me time during a weekend. She told me that during week days, she was very busy in office. She mentioned her son was pursuing Masters in the US and her husband traveled a lot. She had nothing to do on weekends. A very different answer indeed! So we don't know why people want to talk to us or why they don't want to. Our job is to find their preference and follow up accordingly.

One of my customers similarly didn't pick my call. I sent him a message, asking when would be a right time to talk to him. He told me to call him any time after 8 pm. I was surprised again. But with him, anytime you call after 8 pm, he will give you enough time. So the best thing is to ask your client which day, which time, what mode of communication is best to reach him. Some are comfortable on Whatsapp, some are comfortable in calls, and some prefer SMS. Whatever they like, use that mode of communication. The biggest problem is we assume a lot of things and we don't explicitly ask them. We have a separate chapter on Power of Asking.

So, how many times can we follow up? You can follow up till the deal comes to a logical end. Either you should win it or lose it. If you lose it, you should know the reason for the loss. Till then, you should keep following up. Also when you follow up, ask the permission for the next follow up. Say for example, when a customer says currently he cannot decide. Ask him whether you can call him next Friday first half to check with him again. Most probably, he will say yes or he will give you some other date and time. This way, he will not get irritated when you call him next time.

Another research says that the number one quality of top sales people across the globe is follow up. If you see any successful sales people, they will be very very good in follow up.

Key Takeaways:

- 94% of sales people and entrepreneurs don't follow up after 4 times

- By making the call for the fifth time, you are eliminating 94% of your competitors

- 6% of people who follow up more than 4 times win 60% of worldwide business

- Even if customer says don't follow up, you should follow up after giving a gap

- Any day, any time is good for follow up, provided you understand the customer preference

- Understanding the customers' mode of communication will be useful in following up

- All successful sales people will be very good in follow ups

POWER OF ASKING

Research says that the probable reason why you didn't get 8 out of 10 things is because you haven't asked for it. Power of asking is one of my favorite topics in all my sales training sessions. Many participants come back to me and share their success stories.

One such participant called me and told me her success story using this principle.

> Amritha was travelling to Dubai in a very reputed airline. While she was boarding the plane, she asked the airhostess to upgrade her ticket to business class. The airhostess asked her whether she was ready to pay extra for that. Amritha replied that she was not interested to pay extra and requested for a free upgrade. The airhostess politely refused it.
>
> After 10 minutes, before the plane took off, the airhostess came to Amritha and told her that she was very lucky and they are happy to upgrade her to business class. Amritha asked her the reason for the

> free upgrade. The air hostess explained that there was one customer in business class who saw his school friend in the same flight and the school friend was travelling in economy class. He asked whether anybody was ready to swap his business class seat for an economy class seat. And as Amritha **asked** the air hostess about business class seat, she decided to give that offer to her. Amritha was happy to travel in business class for no extra charges.

This is exactly how it works. If you ask for it, the world will give it to you. It is called Law of Attraction. So, will we get everything we ask for? Is there a way to ask? How to ask? Whom to ask? Yes. There are 5 magical ways of asking.

1. Ask as if you expect to get it

What it means is ask with a positive expectation. You can start with people who have already given something to you. It will build your confidence. When you are asking with so much conviction and eagerness, the other party will feel it, and he will be willing to give it to you.

2. Assume you already got it and visualize it

Before asking, assume you already got it. Visualize it. Feel it and then ask for it. Imagine you want to ask for an iphone from your father. Close your eyes and visualize the iphone in your hand. Feel the smoothness of the screen, the clarity of the pictures, quality of the music, the video you are watching, etc. Enjoy those moments and then ask for it. It makes a huge difference in the way you ask. Use this principle in anything you ask for. If you are going for a collection of money from your customer, visualize that he has given you a cheque, and you are holding the cheque and saying thank you. Now open your eyes, go and meet him and ask for payment. You will feel the difference.

3. Ask the right person who can give it to you

You should ask the people who can give it to you. One of my friends was running an e-learning company. He got a big deal from a company. After executing the project for 6 months, his payment got stuck. When he started following up for the payment, he understood that the delivery head had no power in releasing the payment, even though he approves it. He asked the delivery head to connect him to the finance head of the client. Then he started following up with the finance head. He developed a good relationship with the finance head. Finally, he got the money after multiple follow ups. Other vendors who are still following up with the delivery head are still waiting for the payment. You should know whom you should ask.

4. Be clear and specific

You have to be very clear and specific while asking because by asking, you are already making the other party do a favor. If you are not clear in your communication, then you are also asking him/her to think and use his/her brain to understand what you are asking. Then, most probably the other party will reject your ask. You have to ask so clearly and specifically that they should not think about what you are asking. It has to be so easy to them. Then your chance of getting that ask is very high. Say for example, you ask a stranger the time. He just sees his watch and tells you the time. Your ask should be so easy for them.

5. Ask again, again and again

My friend Ilangkumaran, we call him Ik, once went for a movie. It was a Pongal day (Pongal is a festival in Tamil Nadu State, India). Many new films release on Pongal and people love to watch movies on the release day itself. He went with his wife, mother, father and son to the movie. As expected, he didn't get the movie ticket and it was all booked. He remembered my session on power of asking and tried to apply it.

He once again went to the counter and a young girl was issuing the ticket. He asked her again whether he would get 5 tickets; she told him that all tickets were sold out and she couldn't help him. Ik was persistent and said he could wait for some more time and he had come with his family and didn't want to disappoint them. The girl at the counter kept quiet. Ik patiently waited there for 5 more minutes. And again he asked for tickets. He was asking for the third time.

Now, the girl replied she would talk to her manager. Now, Ik was hopeful. After 5 minutes, the manager came inside the counter and the girl explained to him about Ik's request. The manager again refused to issue tickets as it was the first day of the movie. Again, Ik requested him to help. After some time, again when Ik requested, the manager asked him to wait for 5 minutes. Then after 5 minutes, the manager over ruled the system with his password and offered Ik 5 movie tickets. This is the power of asking again and again. When the NO is not strong, you to have patiently wait and keep asking again and again.

Kids below 5 years follow all the above 5 principles. They are very good in using the power of asking. We took my son Krishna, when he was 3 years old, to a mall. After going to a few shops, he asked me to buy him the red doll from the shop. He asked us with a lot of positive expectation. I am sure he already visualized and started playing with the doll in his mind. He asked me, not my wife. If he asked my wife, she would have shouted at him and taken him away. He knew I would not do that. And he was very clear and specific. He wanted that red-colored doll from that shop. And as you know, like any other kid, he asked that doll 100 times in 5 minutes. Finally, we bought that doll for INR 500, which was worth only INR 50 in a roadside shop. The point is, God has given all of us the "Power of Asking," and we lost it when we grew up.

2 books which will help all of us in this context are *The Aladdin Factor* by Jack Canfield and Mark Victor Hansen and *The Success Principles* by Jack Canfield with Janet Switzer. I recommend you read both these books to master this topic. Most of my writings are influenced by these books.

Key Takeaways:

- We would have got 8/10 things in life, if we just ask for it

- There are 5 magical ways for asking

- Ask as if you expect to get it

- Assume you already got it and visualize it

- Ask the right person
- Be clear and specific
- Ask again and again

REFERRALS AND FEEDBACK

Top sales people know that the easiest way to get a new sale is by asking for referrals from the existing client. We have discussed a lot about power of asking in one of the chapters. Asking for referrals is an extension of it.

When to Ask for Referrals

You cannot ask for referrals anytime you want. The best time is the moment you have given a great service and the customer has just sent a thank you note. Within the next 2-3 days, you can meet him and ask for referrals because you are in the good books of him right now. Meet him, spend some time with him and ask for help. You can say that you are looking for more business. If he can help you in connecting with good customers like him, it would be of great help to you. To be precise, convey that you are looking for companies who are in the same or similar industry like his. This will make the work easy for him.

The other best way to ask for referrals is asking your customer after receiving feedback. Once in a while, say once in 3 months or once in 6 months, you can call or meet your customer and ask him for feedback for your work. Some customers may give it; some will not give it. But still, I recommend you ask for it. When they are giving feedback, patiently listen to it. For some of the feedback if you can take immediate action, do take those actions. If some are long-term suggestions, acknowledge that and give your initial thoughts on how you are going to implement it. Then, at this point you can ask for referrals. As you have listened to your customer patiently till now, he will be ready to listen to you now. Use the tactics mentioned in the previous paragraph to ask for referrals.

When You Should Not Ask for Referrals

Never ask for referrals, when there is already an issue going on with your customer. You are currently not in his good books and this is not the time. Solve the issue. Get appreciation and then ask for referrals. When you have just sent a proposal, don't ask for referrals (even if you have already done business with him).

When you know your customer is struggling in his business for various reasons, don't ask for referrals. He is not in a right frame of mind. Also during year ends, during holidays, don't ask for referrals. Also if your pipeline is strong and you already have sufficient leads, which is more than sufficient to handle, then don't ask for referrals because if you ask for referrals and you get them, it's your responsibility to give full attention to them and convert them.

Frequency of Asking Referrals

So, how many times can you ask for referrals? There is no thumb rule here, but definitely you can ask once in a year or once in 6 months. More than the frequency, you should be ready to work on the referrals you receive from your existing customers. That is more important. It is also better to join referral generating organizations like BNI (Business Network International) where asking for referrals is a weekly phenomenon.

Frequency of Asking Feedback

After a major deal is completed and/or service delivered or product supplied, it's better to ask for feedback. Even if you have not done any service to the customer in the recent past, you can ask for feedback once in 6 months or once in 12 months. This may even give you a new business opportunity. By asking feedback, you are telling them that you are ready to listen, you are respecting them, and you are valuing the relationship. These are the messages which reach the customer, and as we all know mind share precedes market share.

Key Takeaways:

- Asking referrals from existing customers is one of the best and easiest ways to generate new business

- When to ask for referrals is very important

- Similarly when not to ask for referrals is also very important

- Asking referrals once in 6 months or once in 12 months is a good practice

- Ask for feedback once a deal is completed and/or service delivered or product supplied

GRATITUDE

Gratitude is a powerful quality which all successful sales people will nurture within themselves. Vidya runs a recruitment firm. A few years back, during the first week of April, she sent a thank you mail to all her customers. In India, the financial year ends by March 31st and the new financial year starts by 1st of April. This was the text of her mail:

"Dear ABCD (name of the customer),

Hope the last financial year was very productive and fruitful for you. Thanks for supporting us in the last financial year. We respect your relationship and want to help you in achieving your success in this financial year as well. Wish you a super successful financial year."

Vidya's real intention is to just wish them success for the financial year. But, to her surprise, all the 100+ clients she wrote to replied wishing her success. 6 of them gave her new business (which was not expected), 12 of them called her for a meeting saying that the meeting was pending for a long time. Imagine customers calling you for a meeting and asking your availability. Out of this 12, 8 gave her business during her meeting with them. Suddenly her pipeline increased and within next 3 months, she had enough work. All of this happened, just by sending one thank you mail. See, what gratitude can bring you, if you are doing it with right intentions.

As we discussed in the chapter Team Handling, any action which is rewarded and recognized will be repeated. If you thank people genuinely from your heart for their help, they will in turn want to help you more. The positive spiral continues.

Similarly, last year on January 1st, based on the data of my company, I created a list of Top 10 people who referred me to customers, or who helped me in getting new business. This list had many of my friends, some of my ex colleagues etc. When I called them and informed them that they are in the Top 10 list of people who gave me more support last year and I want to thank them, they felt very happy. Within the next few weeks, I started getting more referrals from them. My intention was not to get referrals. But you can't avoid the positive spiral which follows once you thank people. What a good situation to be in!

Key Takeaways:

- Gratitude is one of the key characters of top sales people
- When you show gratitude, it is followed by a positive spiral
- New year beginning or new financial year beginning are good times to thank people

REFERENCE BOOKS

1. How to Win Friends and Influence People – **Dale Carnegie**

2. The Success Principles – **Jack Canfield**

3. You can Sell: Results are Rewarded, Efforts Aren't – **Shiv Kera**

4. Be a Sales Super Star – **Brian Tracy**

I thank all the above authors. My writing is greatly influenced by them. I recommend all my readers to buy and read the above books.

www.ingramcontent.com/pod-product-compliance
Lightning Source LLC
Chambersburg PA
CBHW030802180526
45163CB00003B/1130